Animal Stories

James MacPherson

India | USA | UK

Animal Short Stories © 2023

James MacPherson

All rights reserved.

No part of this publication may be reproduced, stored in a retrieval system, or transmitted, in any form or by any means, electronic, mechanical, photocopying, recording or otherwise, without the prior written permission of the presenters.

James MacPherson asserts the moral right to be identified as the author of this work.

Presentation by *BookLeaf Publishing*

Web: www.bookleafpub.com

E-mail: info@bookleafpub.com

ISBN: 9789358316070

First edition 2023

Baa Baa Quack Bleat

Baa Baa Quack Bleat
Any An-i-mal
Yes sir, Yes miss,
Pages full
Poems hereafter
No one the same
All about animals and what they became…

The Hungry Bear

Up in the hills in a cold dark cave
Lived a hungry bear, and food she craved
And so she wandered down the hill
Her empty belly, she sought to fill

As she approached the woods below
She saw a tasty-looking crow
Who flew up high with a flap and a bounce
Just as the bear was about to pounce

The crow called down - who goes there?
And a roar came back, "A hungry bear!"
"So you thought that I would do for starters.
But what say you and I be partners?"

Bear growled "How could you help me?
Other than to be my tea?"
But the clever crow said " I've a hunch,
that I can lead you to your lunch"

So the hungry bear, went where crow led
Trusting what the crow had said
Who landed near a tiny hollow.
"Now here is something you can swallow!"

The bear looked closely in the hole
And saw a tiny little vole
She reached inside and plucked him out
And went to crunch - but heard a shout

"Wait, don't eat me, put me back!
I'd barely be a measly snack!
Why not instead, just let me try,
To help find more to satisfy"

The bear did wonder if the vole
Would even fill a tiny hole
And so decided it was right
To let vole help her in her plight

So now all three went off in search
Bear waiting for the crow to perch
Following her little team
Just then crow stopped above a stream.

The hungry bear then scanned the water
To see where crow and vole had brought her
And spotted just below the surface
Just in fact what was the purpose

She swiped a paw and grabbed a fish
"Finally! The day's first dish"
before she bit, the fish did yelp
And begged the bear that he could help
"If you follow me down river
A hearty meal I shall deliver
One fish will never fill your belly
Plus will make your breath all smelly"

The fish then waited scared and wincing
Hoping he had been convincing
And with that bear released her grip
To let fish join the food-search trip

And so the four; swam, flew and stumbled
As poor bear's empty stomach rumbled
Ahead she saw that they were nearing
A tow path further in the clearing

All four stopped just by a boat
And grazing there a juicy goat
Now this thought bear, is what I need
As her hunger turned to greed

Bear licked her lips prepared to eat
The goat looked up, let out a bleat
And pleaded with the hungry bear
To reconsider his despair

The goat, now mumbling very hurried
"We only taste nice when we're curried!
And you'll get awful stomach bloat
From eating a whole Billy goat!"
The Bear's impatience grew and grew
"Well, what would you all have me do?
I can't eat birds, or fish or meat
But I'm starving and I need to eat!

I've gone without this long already
Maybe I should just turn veggie!"
And at that point they all agreed
That fruit and veg was best indeed

Bear's grateful and surviving troop
A very odd, unlikely group
Led her to a vast lush meadow
With fields and hedges, green and yellow

Trees and bushes filled with berries
Apples, pears and even cherries
So much food there in the offing
Bear in no time, started scoffing

And as her painful hunger eased
The bear admitted she was pleased
She had made friends, was glad to meet them
Happy that she didn't eat them

The Giraffe with the really long scarf

In an African desert a long way away
A Giraffe and a Zebra sat in the shade
For it was the hottest and driest of days
Too hot to graze in the yellowy haze
The heat from the sun was far too much
The golden sand too hot to touch
No clouds at all, just glaring sun
It was just too hot for anyone

The Giraffe and Zebra began to swelter
Wishing they had better shelter
Behind the only trees they'd found
the only trees for miles around
there to share a special date
they both had met to celebrate
The Zebra sang hip-hip hooray
Wishing Giraffe a great Birthday

Zebra dragged a great big box
That he'd hidden in between some rocks
Wrapped in paper end to end
He pushed it forward toward his friend
Excitedly nodding with his head
This is for you the Zebra said
I had it made especially
Giraffe just stared impressively

A tear where the paper overlapped
Keen to get his gift unwrapped
He pulled and ripped at it frantically
until the prize was clear to see
a mass of fabric blue and green
the longest scarf he had ever seen
He held it up, to make quite sure
And then asked Zebra: "What's this for?"

Why on earth did you get me a scarf
We live in the desert, you're having a laugh
there's nothing more pointless to give a giraffe
like a snake some gloves or a parrot a bath
a balloon or a card; those would suffice
plus it's too long, it would go round me twice
Even in winter it doesn't get chilly
Surely you see that this present is silly

The Zebra was sad his friend wasn't happy
Upset his friend was being so snappy
He'd tried to be nice, tried hard to be pleasant
He thought that he'd found a suitable present
But hoped for a bit more gratitude
Instead of this ungrateful attitude
Zebra was hurt and now wasn't sure
that he could be friends with Giraffe anymore
The Giraffe could see that Zebra was sad
And realised that his behaviour was bad
He lowered his head to say to his mate
"I'm sorry Zebra, my present is great!"
I really regret my unpleasant mood
For being so hurtful, ungracious and rude
I'm loving the colours, the green and the blue
Its magnificent size; and that it's from you!

Just then Giraffe had a brilliant thought
A use for the gift that Zebra had brought
He emptied the box and unravelled the scarf
Laid it full length to fold it in half
He folded the fabric, pleat after pleat
Until the Giraffe had created a sheet
He draped it over the tallest tree
To make a large shady canopy

The pair stood happily in the shade
Under the tent that Giraffe had made
Zebra was pleased his friend Giraffe

Was able to use his enormous scarf
Providing cover from the heat
With their stripey coloured sheet
Happy in their own-made den
Happy to be friends again

The Greedy Wildebeest

In the desserts of the Serengeti
No pizzas, burgers or spaghetti
And food is sparse and hard to find
Where most are lean and well streamlined
But one who was more for-tun-ATE
With food served to him on a plate
The most ravenous resident at the zoo
Ate more than the greediest, could get-through

His name was Wilbur - Wilbur East
The zoo's only incumbent Wildebeest
A portly brown lump on skinny legs
Who dreamt of McDonald's, KFC....Greggs
If only he could achieve the feat
Of ordering dinners on just-eat

If he had thumbs or even knew
Just how to use Deliveroo

A carvery, dinner or banquet even
There's not a table he'd be leaving
Breakfast, supper a midnight snack
Afternoon tea or a picnic pack
Any time of day, any type of meal
Eating food was the appeal
All he wanted was a feast
This greedy, hungry Wildebeest

But Wilbur had to recognise
His belly bigger than his eyes
And maybe even contemplate
If his legs could carry all that weight
Perhaps it was the better goal
To lower his cholesterol
Tell his stomach to be quiet
And consider going on a diet

And so the moral of this story
although not dead obligatory
Healthy eating, eat with sense
To avoid becoming too immense
Don't go mad like Wilbur East
And turn out chunky or obese
Or even worse end up deceased
Don't be like that greedy Wildebeest

Seamus who wanted to be Famous

In a bird cage up West a young Parrot perched
Not crackers but fame, this little bird searched
A dream to be famous and be on TV
What Parrot would have, such a stunning CV

His name was Seamus and able to talk
A beautiful voice no hint of a squawk
He'd warble and harmonise sat in his cage
Never tiring of singing, singing for days

Plucky young Seamus was a talented lad
Picking up skills from his Mum and his Dad
A keen little show-man with musical flair
A big, Beaky smile and a tuft of green hair

He was able to sing like a perfect soprano
Through his cage that sat on a big grand piano
The potential already that he would go far
Singing note for note perfect, bar after bar

On days when his owners opened his cage
He'd perch on a shelf like it was a stage
Belting out songs, perfecting each note
Singing tunes straight into the TV remote
His voice was a gift, there was no mistaking
Seamus's voice was simply breathtaking
He'd sing any time, any second or minute
Whatever the song, Seamus could sing it

Only one outcome for talented Seamus
To make it in music and be really famous
But how could he show off his musical knack
Appear in the charts and sing his own track

A song competition would be a good choice
Tho' birds can't do X-Factor or go on The Voice
But to go on TV and showcase his skills
Searching for stardom and new record deals

He was so determined that he'd be a star
He flew out the window, and followed a car
Perched on a bus and headed for town
In search of a crowd that he could astound

Flew down to the street by the main row of shops
Just like a debut on top-of-the-pops
He tried to imagine the first guitar string
Shut his eyes tightly and started to sing

A little crowd formed to hear Seamus croon
But Seamus just carried on singing his tune
More and more people were stopping to hear
Helping the youngster's nerves disappear

He finished the song and people applauded
A week after that all his songs got recorded
A musical agent that day in the town
Just couldn't ignore Seamus' wonderful sound

No longer a make-believe stage in his home
No cage, no restrictions, or fake microphone,
No longer unheard of, nameless and fameless
The Talented Parrot was now Seamus the famous!!

Ducks and Pets

Three little ducks went swimming one day
But how can you tell what those ducks say
When you go to the park and feed them bread
What goes on in a little duck's head
The same for birds and dogs and cats
And all our pets, even rats
So here's some tales of ducks and pets
Shall we read them? Ok let's….

Feeding the Ducks

On days that I have nothing to do
Getting tired of hearing him bark
I take the dog for a walk
and wander down to the park

Through the big metal gates
past the swings and the slide
down the gravelly path
with the hedge on one side

We get to my favourite place
My absolute favourite bit
the bench by the side of the pond
where me and the dog like to sit

I try and bring bread for the birds
hearing the quacks and the clucks
There are pigeons, magpies and gulls
But my favourite is feeding the ducks

The lady ducks tend to be brown
With a bit of dark blue on their tail
The men have pretty green heads
And that's how you know they are male

You'll see them follow each other
Often in couples of two
Quacking away to each other
Doing what ducks always do

But I've noticed something intriguing
I can't unsee how it looks now
They always look like they are lost
And that couple is having a row

We have no idea what they're saying
And I guess, we will never know
But I like to imagine they're asking
passers-by, "Which way do we go?"

But maybe the man-duck refused
To ask for directional aid
And now Mrs Duck is annoyed
For where the both of them strayed

There might be a much better pond
Some ducks apparently know this
somewhere they're fed "posher" bread
maybe the ducks prefer Hovis

So spare a thought for those ducks
who lack navigational skills
And can't ask us for directions
If they only had mouths and not bills…

Little Duckling

Poor little duckling why have you strayed
Getting waylaid
when you should've stayed
Close-by to mumma duck, swam alongside
Followed the river's soft trickly tide
They've headed downstream
and look where you've landed
All by yourself, lonely and stranded
Calling for help at the top of your beak
Making no more than a shrill little squeak

Lucky for you Mum's coming to find
There's no way she'd leave little duckling behind

Who's Tail is that

A little girl watched from where she sat
And thought to herself who's tail is that?
A furry snake poking through the blind
she wondered who was sat behind....

Too impatient, not to wait
She decided to investigate
Hoping to perhaps hear back
She shouted out; who's tail is that?

Who's tail is that, it's far too fat
to be the tail of my pet rat
A rat's tail is all bald and skinny
it can't be her, my rat called Minnie

Who's tail is this, going swish, swish, swish
Too fluffy to be my pet fish
A fishtail would be slippery wet
That tail belongs to a different pet

Who's backside does that there tail belong
Hop the rabbit?...no far too long!
My Rabbit's tail is round and tufty
Unless that tail is my pet Husky

My Dog's tail wags and is quite long
But I'm not so sure, it just seems wrong
The tail I see is not white or grey
It's not my dog there's just no way

That tail is orange like a carrot
It could be Seamus my pet Parrot
But his is feathered and much more flat
I just can't tell who's tail is that?

Just then the girl she heard a sound
At the window was a soft meow
Excitedly the girl cried out
I know the tail, I've worked it out!

I know now just who's tail that is
that swishing length of ginger frizz
So one last time - who's tail is that?
That's the tail of my pet cat

Pets don't like the vets

My cat is called Berlioz, Berli for short
Adopted by chance not paid for or bought
And Berli-cat has a trouble-free life
No worries, no problems, no stress and no strife

Often he sleeps, curled up being lazy
Except random moments he goes a bit crazy
Maybe chasing a bug or a toy round the floor
Or asking to leave, pawing at the backdoor

But one thing he hates, his only regret
Is that infrequent trip to go to the vet
There's nothing that really troubles him more
Than seeing the carry-box out on the floor

He howls and meows all the way on the bus
Like he's-being-kidnapped, making all sorts of fuss
And carries on shouting as soon as we're there
I sit embarrassed, on the waiting room chair

Once with the vet, now he wants to stay put
Clinging-on to the box with each paw and each foot
Straight on the scales now sullen and quiet
Whilst the vet says "perhaps he should go on a diet"

The vet checks his fur and looks at his teeth
Feeling all round, on the top, underneath
The vet turns away searching a drawer
Now Berli eyes up his escape to the floor

Then one little injection in the back of the neck
No pain and no blood, not even a speck
And with that it's over this awful ordeal
All that fuss over something he didn't even feel

No trouble now getting him back in the box
Quick as a flash, straight out the blocks
Waiting to leave, instinctively knowing
We're done at the vets. It's time we were going

As I carry him out back into reception
I realise that Berli is not the exception
None of the pets look particularly pleased
At the thought of being prodded and squeezed

It occurred to me then, most pets are alike
If given the choice – they'd say "on your bike!"
I'd rather not go, let's stay at home, let's
Because pets mostly don't like a trip to the vets

Diddy the Goat intro

There once was a small goat called Diddy
So excitable, and so very giddy
He bucked and he bleated
Any time he was greeted
If he ever wore pants they'd be skiddy

Diddy the Goat

Everything was still that day on the farm
The animals asleep curled up in the barn
But just then the sun just started to show
On the horizon; an orangey glow

The chicken coop was the first place to stir
where feathery movement began to occur
ruffling feathers, kicking and strutting
the hen-house filled with cooing and clucking

The sun now appearing low in the sky
The whole of the farm hearing the cry
No-one could ignore or try to sleep through
The loud piercing shriek of cock-a-doodle-do

The poor sleeping farmer, fell out of bed
The sound of the cockerel rang in his head
He never got used to his daily alarm
Which woke every animal up on the farm

The farmer stood up and pulled on his wellies
The whole of the farmyard had rumbling bellies
The sheep were all bleating, the cows all mooo'd
They all wanted breakfast, impatient for food

Two massive buckets, of food on each arm
The farmer hurriedly feeding the farm
In such a rush he'd forgot to get dressed
He was dashing about in his pants and a vest

After scattering the pens with scraps, swill and oats
and tending the sheep, the cows and the goats
The farmer felt cold from his head to his toes
And that's when he saw he was missing his clothes

The farmer's dog Shep had started to laugh
As the embarrassed old man ran down the path
The pigs also chuckled and so did the crows
He hurried inside to put on his clothes

But that wasn't the worst thing to happen that day
One of the animals had managed to stray
The clumsy old farmer had made a mistake
And forgotten to lock one of the gates

One of the goats, the smallest of all
A pygmy called Diddy coz he was so small
Had managed to slip through a crack in the gate
And couldn't believe that he had escaped

Diddy goat skipped and bucked at the thought

Of venturing out, without getting caught
He knew he would miss his friends on the farm
Surely seeing the world, couldn't do any harm...

So off Diddy skipped with a baa and a bleat
Excited at the thought of who he might meet
And all the adventures, the things he would see
Escaping the farmyard and being set free

Diddy's search for the city

So a naughty, mischievous, curious, goat
had found his way out of his home
with little black horns and a mottled brown coat
and a beard on his chin just a tad overgrown

Although small for a goat he would never grow
bigger
Appropriately he'd been named Diddy
A fully grown adult with a childish figure
You'd have thought he was still just a kiddie

So he hopped and he skipped away from the farm
from which he had just departed
the sun shone bright and the weather was calm
his adventure had only just started

Diddy decided he fancied a trip
To a hustley bustley city
he carried on going with a hop and a skip
until he met Little Grey Kitty

She was there by the path, curled up in the grass
having an afternoon nap
excuse me said Diddy, "Where abouts is the city?"
"It's quite far!"; yawned the sleepy young cat

You might want to think about catching a ride
On a bus or a train or a tractor
It's too far to walk or to skip or to hop
the distance is quite a big factor

Diddy said thanks but carried on walking
Past miles of wide open space
he stopped in his tracks, hearing a rustle
and then saw a rather long face

Just there in a field stood by the gate
a horse was eating some hay
Diddy asked nicely, "Which way to the city?"
Naaaayyyy…. that's a LONG WAY away

The horse almost laughed at Diddy's request
The nearest city was far
He shook his big head saying; "I think it best
If you were to travel by car"

Diddy said thanks but stuck to his mission
Clicking along down the road
He needed more help toward his ambition
And then spotted old Mr Toad

"Excuse me Toad'y"....Diddy enquired
But I've asked the horse and the kitty
"I've been on this path for miles and miles,
Please say I'm now close to the city?"

The grumpy old Toad puffed out his neck
And huffed… "Is this a joke?"
Follow the road as far as it goes
He managed to say with a croak

Poor tired Diddy stuck to his task
His hoofs clicking step after step
Fed up and weary and desperate to ask
….If he was even getting close yet

Just when he'd gone a little bit further
He spotted a bird in the sky
Bucking and bleating, Diddy tried hard
To catch the flying bird's eye

The crow swooped down to a nearby post
And let out a loud piercing squawk
"Where little goat, do you think you are going?
It's quicker to fly than to walk"

Diddy was panting so tired from his quest
And asked the crow to take pity
"Please Mr Crow, please say if you know
I'm trying to get to the city"
The bird lifted his wing and pointed ahead
"I really don't know why you care
But you've not far to go," ….cackled the crow
"In fact it is just over there!"

Diddy was desperate to see where he meant
He ran through some trees to a clearing
Then he gazed in delight, at the wonderful sight
In the distance – The City appearing

He'd finally made it all by himself
Though his legs felt heavy and sore
Tired from walking but over the moon
Diddy couldn't wait to explore….

Diddy's good deed

The city was filled with noise, lights and smells
And a faint background noise playing "Jingle Bells"
Diddy had arrived in the bustling place
Trotting proudly along with a smile on his face

The shops were all dressed with Christmas attire
Experiencing shopping was Diddy's desire
And during December with so much to see
Every shop window a twinkling tree

But it seemed every door that Diddy goat went
"No goats allowed!" and out he was sent
He snuck in a few behind people's bags
But struggled to read any items' price-tags

He hadn't thought through that shopping is hard
When you haven't got money, cash or a card
And no one allows goats in their stores
Expelled every time and sent back outdoors

So now poor old Diddy was stuck in the city
With not much to do, which he thought was a pity
After all the effort to get himself there
Where now he thought, I don't know where

There wasn't in fact much there at all

For one such as Diddy, a goat who's so small
So busy it seemed, minding everyone's feet
Every so often he'd let out a bleat

Just then as he walked, he did double-take
Convinced that in fact he had made a mistake
But staring right back, one of his own
A goat just like Diddy, he wasn't alone

He jigged and he bleated, at his new acquaintance
And waited excitedly, showing some patience
With nothing forthcoming from his newfound friend
Actually a toy, it turned out in the end

Diddy worked out that the goat wasn't real
Looked up and noticed a little girl's heel
She was looking back and pointing at Diddy
Maybe she dropped it, possibly? Did she?

The little girl's Mum was carrying her
Into the distance they started to blur
What best to do, Diddy didn't quite know
But made the decision….just go Diddy GO!

He weaved and he winded between people's feet
The same direction as the girl down the street
Desperately looking for the girl and her Mum
Could feel his heart beating so hard like a drum

Just as he came to a big open square
He spotted the girl, they'd stopped over there
By a big Christmas Tree and what looked like Santa
He slowed his galloping down to a canter

And with some relief, walked up and stopped
Gave back to the girl the toy that she dropped
Her Mum never noticed this wonderful deed
Performed by Diddy the tiny young steed

But Diddy took pride in what he'd achieved
Trotting away feeling terribly pleased
The girl mouthed to Diddy, "Many thanks! Merry Christmas"
And satisfied Diddy went back to his business

Diddy concluded and started to see
That it could be the city "isn't for me"
And headed away from the busy town centre
Plotting the path to his next great adventure

Winter and Christmas Poems
Intro

Rudolph the red-nosed reindeer
Winter poems I enclose
Panda's and Christmas stories
Polar Bears with frozen toes
Who wants to be a reindeer
Something I cannot deduce
Who wants to be poor Rudolph
Well in actual fact there is a moose…

What do Polar Bears do for fun

What do Polar Bears do for fun
They can't go to the park and play in the sun

I imagine they watch the 'Northern Lights'
Or play in the snow having snowball fights…
Perhaps they shop for thermal socks
Or get to play 'fetch' with an Artic Fox

Maybe they all go to Eskimo fairs
Or sit around talking on ice-sculpted chairs
They might build dens somewhere snowy and rocky
Or learn how to skate and play ice-hockey
They might gaze through the ice waiting for fish
Crossing their paws and making a wish

No bears by the pool dipping their toes in
Coz all the swimming pools tend to be frozen
I doubt they would need to put ice in their drinks
Or have any trouble finding ice-skating rinks

They wouldn't drive cars but instead snowmobiles
With skis on the bottom, no good having wheels
No need for fridges to keep their food cold
Their bread and their cheese would never grow mould

But really hot weather could cause them an issue
It has to stay cold or it might melt their igloo
The ones that live in round frozen houses
With their natural fur-coats and thick woolly trousers

Fishing through holes they've made in the ground
Hungry seals watch them, not hanging around

After dinner, then where might a Polar Bear go
To Wolf-Karaoke; Or a Penguin disco
To maybe watch whales, play in icy lagoons
Or sit round the fire singing Christmassy tunes

Those bears who live in the ice and the snow…
How do they have fun? Well now you know!

Who wants to be Rudolph anyway

Who wants to be Rudolph and have a red nose
Go all the cool places that Rudolph goes
Every year with such a significant role
In Santa's amazing yearly goal
Presents and boxes and toys to deliver
Best job in the world – a happiness giver

Who wants to be Dasher or Dancer or Vixen
Or a name hard to spell like Rudolph or Blitzen
Who wants to fly, through the air at top speed
Or stand around waiting on a cold Christmas eve
Whilst some jolly fat bloke hops rooftop to chimney
I really do tend to view it all dimly

Who wants to be Donner, Prancer or Comet
Unnecessarily showy, I just want to vomit

It really is quite outrageous and stupid
Calling a reindeer Rudolph or Cupid
I mean what do they do the rest of the year
That set them apart from the poor other deer

Is it really, entirely so special a job
And that's not just me being a snob
But I have got hooves and antlers the same
Maybe I'd like to try, the delivery game
I've been overlooked from what I deduce
Why only reindeers and why not a Moose
Where can I apply and put myself forward
Not to be difficult or make things awkward
I just think it's unfair only 9 get a go
Tell me the criteria just so I know
I can change my name to Dancey or Flasher
Anything to be a Reindeer gatecrasher!

Dear Mr Claus consider us Mooses
For next year's transport between all them Hoo'ses
Can call on my friends Marty and Mike
Can come up with as many Moose as you like
Just give us a go at pulling the sleigh
On that magical night before Christmas Day

The Panda who didn't believe in Santa

Winter had fallen on London zoo
Around the enclosure a bustling queue
Children and parents all having a gander
Desperate to glimpse a rare giant panda

The bears took no notice of the jostling crowds
Ignoring the oohs and the aahs and the wows
Happily chomping on their fruit-and-veg diet
They knew that tomorrow the Zoo would be quiet

For it was Xmas eve; 2 panda cubs sat
Munching their lunch and having a chat
1-year-old brothers, from a litter of two
One was named Bam the other called Boo

One asks the other, "Do you believe?"
Halfway through a mouthful of leaves
What do mean??... Bam says to Boo
Do you think Santa will visit our Zoo?

I don't think he's real, Boo quickly replied
The elves and the reindeers; I think it's all lies
We don't have a chimney, don't even have stairs
And what makes you think, he delivers to bears

Bam couldn't believe his brother was right
Angrily saying "you just wait til tonight!..."
The rest of the day they both played alone
The zoo became empty as people went home

Nighttime rolled round and calmness descended
Poor little Bam was still feeling offended
He couldn't believe there's no Father Christmas
And he wouldn't receive the gifts on his wish-list

The other young Panda also was moping
He meant what he'd said, but was secretly hoping
he still didn't trust in Santa's existence
Despite hearing Sleigh-Bells far in the distance

Suddenly something appeared in the sky
A funny shaped object appearing to fly
The closer it got the quicker it flew
And it looked to be heading straight for the zoo

Bam screamed to his brother "pretend you're asleep!"
Shut your eyes tightly, don't even peep!
It's definitely Santa but make no mistake
He won't leave us presents if he thinks we're awake
Boo's eyes were still shut and he felt himself yawning
He didn't dare risk getting up before morning
Both him and his brother laid there quite still
Both content in the fact knowing Santa is real

The next day both Pandas opened their eyes
12 carrots were missing and several mince pies
but left in their place, a number of gifts
All marked; Merry Christmas, love Santa xx
(kiss kiss)

The End poem

Was the night before Christmas and all through the zoo
Not a sound could be heard, not a moo or a coo
For everyone knew that maybe it's true
T'was the night that Santa Claus passes through

So make sure you're sleeping and snuggled up tight
If you want him to come on that magical night
Then try to be good and kind through the year
Or else not much chance that he will stop here

A good place to finish this book here I feel
About all the animals, both made-up and real
They would say goodbye; I'm sure that they would
If able to talk, if maybe they could
To us it would just be a quack, baa, meow
And that's where we'll leave the stories for now

The End

Milton Keynes UK
Ingram Content Group UK Ltd.
UKHW021003070524
442340UK00016B/657